The **Oldie**
BOOK OF CARTOONS
1992–2009

Chosen by
Richard Ingrams

This compilation first published in 2009
by Oldie Publications Ltd

65 Newman Street, London W1T 3EG
www.theoldie.co.uk

ISBN-10: 1-901170-08-X

ISBN-13: 978-1-901170-08-5

A catalogue record for this book
is available from the British Library

Printed by Thanet Press

Introduction

MANY READERS would not admit it but the first thing they do with a magazine like *The Oldie* is to flick through it to look at the cartoons. If that is true, as I think it is, then the cartoons assume enormous importance. (It is also true, in the case of *The Oldie*, that the cartoons give rise to more angry letters than any other feature of the magazine.)

Yet cartoonists seldom get any credit for this – not that I imagine they harbour any resentment on that account. They are for the most part modest, retiring and even reclusive characters. In many cases, although I have been familiar with their work for many years, I have never clapped eyes on them or even spoken to them on the phone. I have noted before how many of them seem to live in the North of England. Almost all of them are male and the cartoon world tends to be a very male one in which men are having a hard time, as in the classic cartoon situations: a man wrecked on a desert island or crawling across the desert in search of water, a man standing on a window ledge about to commit suicide. Domestically life is just as dire… His wife doesn't understand him and if he goes out for a night on the tiles she will be waiting for him behind the door, rolling pin at the ready. No wonder he is frequently to be seen on a psychiatrist's couch.

Possibly this melancholy bias springs from the cartoonists' own circumstances. It is a difficult life. The financial rewards are not great and ninety per cent of their jokes are destined to be returned with a polite rejection slip. In the meantime the number of outlets is shrinking year by year.

In spite of all this, the quantity and quality of cartoons submitted to *The Oldie* is gratifyingly high and there is a wide variety of styles, some elaborate, some simple. You can usually tell which of them have been to art school and which of them are self-taught.

This collection covers seventeen years, so not surprisingly we have to record that some of the best cartoonists featured here have died. I mourn especially Terence Parkes (Larry) and Ged (Ged Melling), who contributed almost exclusively to *The Oldie* in the final years. But what is so encouraging is that new talents – not always young ones – keep emerging to take their place.

For me it has always been a great pleasure to select cartoons and being by nature a somewhat morose individual I am especially grateful to those inventive men – and women! – who have given me so many good laughs over the years.

RICHARD INGRAMS

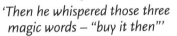
'Then he whispered those three magic words – "buy it then"' IV

HU

'How do you slip "What's your favourite hymn?" into the conversation?' GR

'We have CCTV footage of your entire life' HO

'You may feel a slight excruciating agony' IB

'I get the feeling you don't like that dog very much'

'Let us play'

'I'll take it'

'Has someone stolen your car?' PA

'It's just what Big Harry
would have wanted' IV

'You don't grumble so much these days. Is everything all right?'

'Okay! You can treat me privately...' **GZ**

'Go on, you can do it! Think misery!' **NB**

'They grow up fast, don't they?'

ND

'Shan't be long, Fred, I'm just nipping home for a cigarette'

'Don't try and get fresh with me'

'Normally it doesn't bother me, only this morning I heard them mention our names'

'Can't we just draw a line under it and move on?'

'He's not seeing anyone today' DA

'And it shall come to pass, great Caesar,
you shall have a salad named after you...' LI

'Hurry up – I've only got time
for a soundbite' HB

'It's bad news I'm afraid, Mr Hall. I've been having an affair with your wife'

AS

IN

ND

'Have you any idea how many sea turtles have been trapped
in shrimp nets while we've been enjoying ourselves?'

'Uh-oh, fly topping. You've given
me Spiderman's order again'

'I've decided to go for set-aside'

DA

COX

'They're not organic really, I just throw earth on them and put the price up'

RL

'I like it, it's abrasive...'

SW

MON DRIAN

GE

GONE TO
BE FAMOUS
BACK IN
15 MINUTES

BE

'Hello, Guinness Book of Records? We've
got sixteen men on a dead man's chest' MI

After all we are
a Democracy.

Ssh.

GR

23

'I caught her running away
to join the media circus' RT

'What does it say, Eric?
And don't upset me!' CW

WOODCOCK WC

24

'It doesn't have to be this way, Harry. We could attend couples' counselling'

ITEM: 2·10
CASH: 5·00
CHANGE: 2·90

SAY:
'THERE YOU GO'

Reading

'Within what sort of time frame do you anticipate completion?'

'That's all well and good, Peters, but have you
forgotten that today is "tacky Hawaiian shirt Friday"?'

'Well now I know why this cruise was cheap'

'Have you noticed how the security guards seem to follow you around the room?'

'If only he spent as much time battling evil-doers as he does guys who make fun of his tights'

'I've been shopping all day — my fingers are killing me'

'It's amazing what they can do these days'

28

'I'm bitter. At what stage do I become twisted as well?'

BREAKDOWN RECOVERY

29

'I think his walking out on me is just another building block in our relationship'   ND

'Right hand down a bit'   RT

'Look, I didn't know this bloke from Adam – could we skip the Eulogy and move on to "Abide With Me"?'

'It's all right for you. You won't have to go through the grieving process'

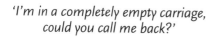

'I'm in a completely empty carriage, could you call me back?'

'There's a space!'

'Hello, I'm kicking a can across the country to promote aimlessness. Care to sponsor me?' **ND**

'Enjoy' **IV**

'Mum, where do we put the rubbish?'

'If you're happy and you know it, clap your hands'

you've forgotten
you already came back
for what you forgot

GED

'Your mother's a keen supporter
of assisted suicide'

GZ

'Hi, I'm in a two-minute silence...'

'I'd hate to see you go away empty-handed'

ND

'Sorry I'm late – I ran into some
traffic on the way home'

ML

'Remember the good old days when
we were the opium of the masses?'

KP

'Long time no see' **ACE**

'I did the decent thing, left him in the library with a loaded revolver, and he sold it on eBay' **RE**

'We wall-papered your room while you were away at university...' **GZ**

'I didn't get around to putting the words on'

PI

ROB

40

'That's our winter fuel allowance well spent'

WOULD YOU LIKE
A FLAKE IN IT?

'Oops, missing you already'

'Don't read too much into it, Mr Perkins, it's just a hole in the roof'

'So she said, "Either that shed goes or I go"'

'So when does the feeling kick in?'

'It's good to get out of uniform'

45

'And at the end of that round, Mr Bell, you've proved that
you're a sad little man whose only interest in life is Henry VIII'

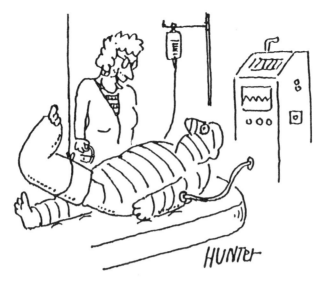

'You should have known I meant "left" when I said "right"'

'You haven't met your merriness performance target'   BP

'Which is the oven?'   NLD

'Would you like me to throw that in the river for you, Sir?'   ROB

48

'Thomas has two computers, two mobile phones
and a Blackberry but no friends to communicate with'

ROB

'Okay, okay! I agree to run the anti-bullying initiative!'

GZ

CHARITY SHOP

'...and who wants to be the store detective today?'

HS

'Excuse me, I just need to get some matches to keep my eyes open'

TH

51

'The Double Deluxe gets both of you upstairs before you can forget why you're going' McN

'Local character with a fund of interesting stories. Buy me a pint and I'll clear off'

'I haven't seen you at church recently'

'Don't overdo it'

'No, dear, I do not think it's time we Homo
sapiens apologised to the Neanderthals'

'My friends!'

'Ah, Osborne, please take a seat, make yourself comfortable' CMA

'You've been distant lately' ND

'He's trying to kick-start the housing market'

'Sure, I got my people to talk to your people –
turned out they were the same people'

'You think you've got problems'

GOD, HAVEN'T YOU GOT A MOBILE YET?

BT

'Goodnight, Nanook. Great housewarming party'

'Can you just relax for me, Mr Watson?' AD

'No, Jeremy, you may not bite me on the neck to see if I turn into one of the undead' RJ

'Here comes the bill'

'Mum, lovely to see you, come in'

SCREECH

COURTESY CAR

'When shall we three meet again? ... When, when, when.'
'I've got a window Tues pm.' 'I'm good.' 'No can do.' 'No?
How's Friday look?' 'Check.' 'Sorry. Thursday's open.' 'Next week?'...

'Would you like me to eat that for you, Sir?'

'This is reality TV – can't you swear a bit more?'

'A couple of suits to see you, Sir'

MINOTAUR

'You can't go in – he's an endangered species!'

'Dad, why do they call us "Travellers"?'

'Can't you sex it up a bit?'

'... a big thank you to all you lovely people out there'

Happiness is enjoying your depression

GED

GED

'WICKED!'

AS

'Personally, I'd recommend a bit of self-restraint, you fat bastard'

'Well, okay, but only if it advances the plot'

STOP! DO NOT ATTEMPT TO MOVE HIM

'So this is limbo'

'Don't I get a receipt?'

'We'll have to leave it there...'

HO

HS

'I can't relax in the country, there aren't any shops'

MIC

ABANDON HOPE
ALL YE WHO
PRESS ENTER
HERE.

Spittle SP

MM

'Stop! Misunderstood victim of an uncaring society!'

'Don't even think of comparing me
to a summer's day, you bastard' RT

'Got anything in gangland?'

PA

'...and now can we have one of the bridegroom's parents?'   RA

'Mmmm, these appetite suppressants are really moreish...'   CO

'Next door have just put orange peel in the wrong bin'   RL

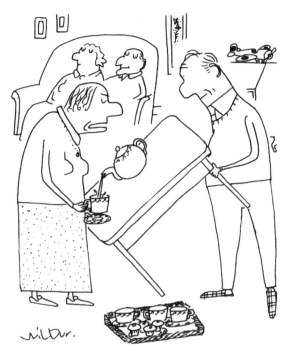

'Next time, remember to put the lid back on the Superglue'   WI

'My husband eats like a bird – do you have any regurgitated insects?'   ND

BK

CRAMER.

CR

'The doctor said I'd got to get out more'

'I see Ingersoll's still testing drugs on himself'

'Oh my God – and she belongs to Friends of the Earth!'

'Whatever...'

'Here's a March special: a five-day "Scatter His Ashes" cruise'

'Got anything in the
Diplomatic Corps, baldy?'

'I think I'll check on how Bob's presentation went'

'No, Clive, that's the fish knife!'

ROB

TA

'... £150,000 ... Sold to the gentleman
in the Napoleon uniform with
a banana stuck in his ear'

MT

'Are we nearly there yet, Dad?'

'Good news, Sir, someone's stolen the Hockney'

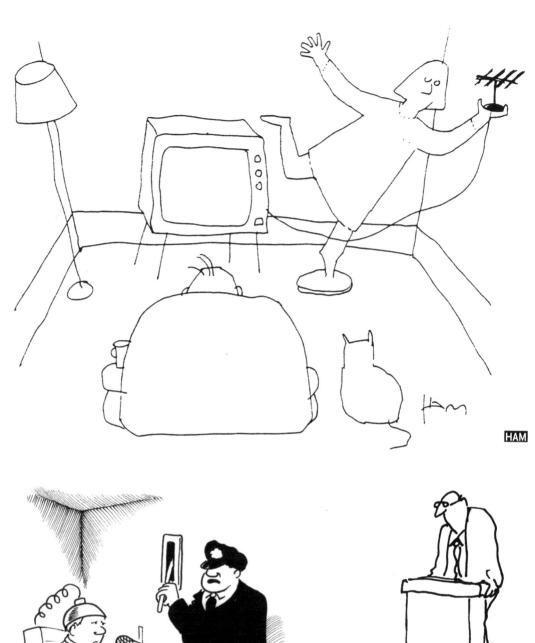

'Your screams may be
recorded for training purposes'

ALL MY OWN
BULLSHIT.

'Polonius, do you mind if I give you a damn good kicking first? We've got a bus-load of football fans in'

'Sorry I'm late. What with Thursday being the new Friday, I thought it was Saturday'

'Don't eat all the peanuts'

'Remind me – am I getting up or going to bed?'

'We'd like to send the chef
an insulting text message'

'Dad, what's an envelope?'

'Enough! The mooing is no longer funny'

'I expect that first you'll want to visit the little boys' room'

93

'It's for you'

'Do you mind if I smoke?'

'... and you're fired as well'

'Champagne for one,
what a saddo'

'Now, what did I come in here for?'

'I'm afraid we're going to have to let you go'

'Mummy, can't we go to
Tesco like everyone else?' GZ

'Is this one dead?' IV

'This is all there is, minus a small service charge'

'Don't you think you're a bit
over-dressed for a first date?'

'Would you care for something from
the healthier lifestyle trolley?'

What you must realise is . . .
that farmer's wife is a very sick person

GED

'Hi, I'm on the piss'

'You could at least leer occasionally' GR

'I'm sexing up my confessions' HB

'Dinner is served!' RA

'He's getting the short, sharp shock'

DA

RAMBLERS ANONYMOUS

'Hi, my name's Dave and I'm a compulsive rambler'

ROB

'And how long have you felt inferior, Mother Superior?'

'By the way, how's your mother these days?'

106

'... but I'm encouraged by their use of renewable energy'

TOY OUTFITS

VACUOUS MEDIA CELEBRITY

'I'd love to know what you do all day in that damn shed' **PAK**

'It's simple: you bully me, I sue, and we split the damages' **JO**

'Fish? No, television screen sizes'

'Let's talk about this, Hilary! There must be another way to meet the council tax demand' NI

'What can I get you, apart from excited?' PA

'Come on, Dr Watson, haven't you got Holmes to go to?'

'He watches it religiously'

'I'm just updating your records...'

Men are from Mars, women are from Venus

Gays are from Brighton

GED

Russell

'This adverse reaction to treatment is just nature's way of telling us that we don't know what's wrong with you'

'I understand it was a tremendous falling out'

ND

'He's not big on suggestions'

LO

It's a lovely way to go

GED

BIRTWISTLE

'There's no need to switch off your mobile phone'

'Waiter, there's some soup in his hair'

'We've done it – we've beaten the record for number of lay-offs set just last year!'

'Can you assure me that no animals were harmed
during the production of this lamb chop?'

'Not now, Henderson, that will have to wait until "Any Other Business"'

'In case of emergency, the person sitting next to you may act as a food source'

'Scissors – I win'

STRESS COUNSELLOR

DIG YOUR OWN

'...and what did the barber say when you called him thick?'

'The new vicar's very much a traditionalist'

'Have you got something suitable for kicking after a hard day at the office?'

'Did you remember to floss?'

'Stand well clear of the door!'

*'It's the inscription on Dad's tombstone.
He won't let Mum put "miserable, tight-fisted old bastard"'*

BT

BR

BY

'I plan to be filthy rich. I'm halfway there already'

'Mum, hi... It's bad news, he's got the all clear'

'Attila the Hun. Do you have a problem with that?'

'Goodness me! Have you seen the salt content in this?' PAK

'They're wildly expensive and excruciatingly painful – I'll take them'

DO

'I worry about the gradual erosion of Christianity, Archbishop...'

BE

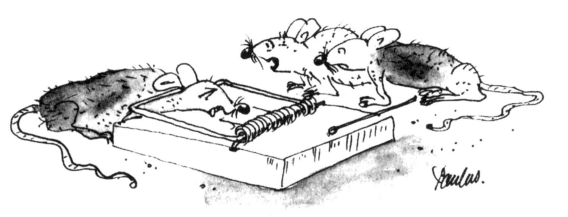

'I'd say he's critical but stable'

PA

'We'll see if there is something we can get you for the pain'

ND

133

'We must do something about
the timing of your grunt'

'Smacking or non-smacking?'

'They should bring back Flower Power – that'd teach 'em'

'Heinz or Campbell's?' **SP**

AE

'We thank you, Lord, for that which we are about to receive, excepting, perhaps, the trace amounts of naturally occurring carcinogens that, in your mysterious way, you've included in the turkey and bread stuffing'

ND

'I don't think Charlie has got used to these automobiles yet'

'This always happens when you meet someone from Friends Reunited'

'I suppose if you really must have a second opinion, I could change my mind' PAN

'My wife told me to tell you to sort yourself out' CAZ

'I would just like to read out a few text messages...'

'There you go, Gentlemen. 2.8 units and 2.3 units. Please drink sensibly...'

'...and when you awake you'll believe my fees to be extremely reasonable'

'We've just moved into your catchment area'

BILL PROUD

'Ignore him, he's after scraps'

143

'I'll have what he had'

'Now look what you've done'

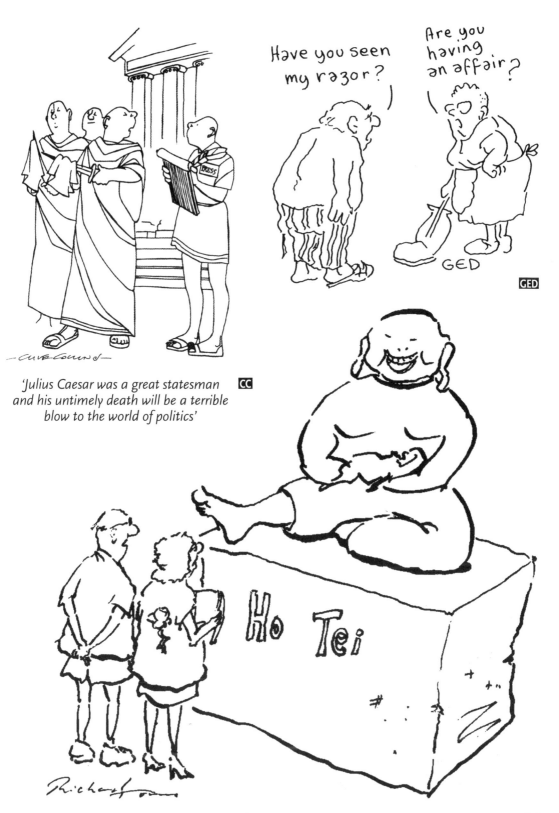

'Julius Caesar was a great statesman and his untimely death will be a terrible blow to the world of politics'

Have you seen my razor?

Are you having an affair?

GED

'I can't believe it's not Buddha'

Ho Tei

'And now a look at tomorrow's front pages. The Telegraph leads with
ULTIMATE MAKEOVER GUIDE, while the Mail has A FANTASTIC NEW YOU...'

'Remind me, Miss Jones, am I hiring or firing?' HU

'Your co-directors wish you a speedy recovery by a vote of 3 to 2' LAW

'He used to be a great stand-up' RT

'We are gathered here today to witness the marriage of
Jez and Lucy over her father's dead body'

'I think they want us to leave'

'You say "Boo", she wets herself'

'I thought we could freeze it...'

'Oh so you do, do you?'

'Could you spare a cup of Valium?'

'Ever made it with a widget salesman?'

'Crazy bitch! I told you never to call me at the office!'

'And as each part of your body relaxes, I want you to focus on those powerful images of peace and serenity... The opening flower, the dew on the leaves...'

'Oh, and your father has been named and shamed'

'This old man – did he play "knick-knack" on other places besides your knee?'

'Hurry up! It's that awful woman you can't stand'

'Nobody's noticed yet'

come on you buggers,
get a bloody move on

'Honoria likes to talk to the plants to encourage them'

'I sometimes think we'd enjoy Eastenders more if we got a telly'   **AE**

'On a day like this, one hardly needs nipple clamps'   **ND**

'Don't disturb your father, he's dog tired'

'Start again, Ned. You were in tune'

'I'm going out to drum up some more business'

'Good morning! My name's Julian and I'll be your torturer today!'

'Come in – Herbert's just watching the fridge defrost' **RL**

'Not bad, but I want to hear more disdain when you say "Nothing I can do about it"' **NI**

'Another 500 quid ensures that the pall-bearers look suitably mournful' **AR**

'Customer enquiry – which bits are working today?'   SA

'I just don't hear the sound of barrels being scraped and that worries me'

'Shall we turn the extractor fan down a bit?'

'Permission to write some poetry, Sir?'

'Frankly, your bum looks big in anything'

'I like the way it draws the eye away from your face'

IV

'Well, Doctor, will I live long enough to sue the hospital?'

you make drawing badly
look easy

GED

'I must ask you to be very long-winded, please'

'Oh, and your ex-wife called'

EXCUSE ME, ONE OF YOUR COWS HAS FOULED THE FOOTPATH!

'Maybe it's nature's way of telling you to slow down?'

HS

WARNING
PEOPLE
WITH
CLIPBOARDS
OPERATE
IN THIS
AREA

GEOFF
HURTON

GH

'Which one's the cardiac arrest?'

HU

'Hey, nice pad'

RS

PASSPORTS

TEN WIVES OR LESS

WA

'Your leg, Cap'n – the men want an assurance that it comes from
a certified renewable source of non-endangered hardwoods'

'If that's the wife, tell her I've not been in'   MW

'Your CV is full of lies.
When can you start?'   ES

one of the great
joys of my life
is turning off
the radio

GED   GED

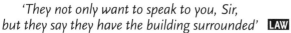
'They not only want to speak to you, Sir,
but they say they have the building surrounded' **LAW**

KJL

'George, please – not your humanitarian award!' ND

'Who shall I say is crawling?' KP

'Dad left home when I was three.
He just never got very far' LO

'She wants to speak to the organ grinder' PAR

'I want to lure ships to their doom' CAZ

'My doctor said I needed to spend more
time outside, so I've started smoking' ACE

'They leave a radish on your pillow'

'Is anything up with Gerald? He seems a bit distant'

'I've found the mini-bar'

'He died doing what he loved the most – shooting it out with the cops'

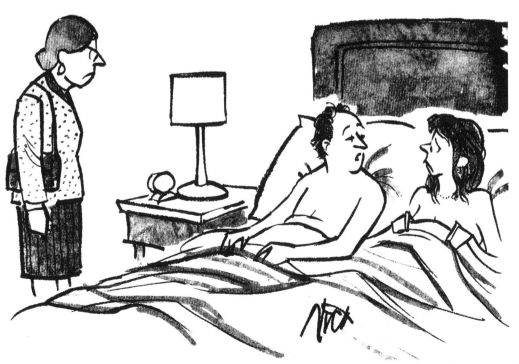

'You're in charge of scheduling, Jessica – how long has this been going on?'

'I'm sorry, but according to my database you're just one sugar'

'New trousers, Sir? What chest size are we?' ML

'What goes with a flaming argument?' PA

'But – and it's a very big but...'

'I've wired the email to the toaster'

'Sorry, cod's extinct today'

187

'And have my boys washed their hands?'

'You've caught us at a bad time. Can I call you back?'

HOW FAR DOWN IS ONE REQUIRED TO DUMB, MINISTER?

STAMP.

'Now my personal favourite: market research shows a very
positive response from the general public to this image'

Glossary of cartoonists

ACE	Tony Eden
AD	Addison
AE	A Exton
AR	Alan Ralph
AS	A J Singleton
AU	Austin
BAK	Barry Knowles
BE	Bernie
BK	Philip Berkin
BL	Blot
BP	Bill Proud
BR	Bill Round
BS	R Besley
BT	Bill Tidy
BY	Bailey
CAZ	Caz
CC	Clive Collins
CL	Cluff
CM	Chris Madden
CMA	Christopher Mackenzie
CO	Colin Wheeler
COX	Cox
CR	Jon Cramer
CW	Colin Whittock
DA	Darling
DD	David Dutton
DLN	de la Nougerede
DO	Dorrance
ES	E Smith
FI	F Jefferies
FR	Alan Freiesleben
GE	George Craig
GED	Ged
GG	Gordan Gurvan
GH	Geoff Hurton
GR	G T Riach
GV	Guy Venables
GZ	Grizelda

HA	Huw Aaron
HAM	Ham Khan
HB	Hugh Burnett
HE	Hewison
HO	Holland
HS	Honeysett
HU	Hunter
IB	Ian Baker
IN	Ines
ION	Ionicus
IV	Ivor
JAG	Jag
JE	Jelliffe
JM	Julian Mosedale
JO	Jorodo
KC	Keith Courtney
KE	Kelly
KJL	K J Lamb
KL	Tom Kleh
KN	Knife
KP	Ken Pyne
LA	Larry
LAW	Lawry
LB	Les Barton
LI	Liz Kneen
LM	Lynne Marie Clarke
LO	Lowe
Mc	McLachlan
McA	McArdle
McN	McNeill
ME	Kieran Meehan
MI	Midge
MIC	Mico
MJ	Meyrick Jones
ML	Mark Lewis
MM	Mike Mosedale
MT	Mike Turner
MW	Mike Williams

MZ	Mazurke
NAF	Andy McKay
NB	Neil Bennett
ND	Nick Downes
NLD	Neil Dishington
NI	Nick Hobart
PA	Paulus
PAK	Pak
PAN	Pantelis Palios
PAR	Parker
PAT	Pat
PE	Pearsall
PI	Pidge
PW	Philip Warner
RA	Derek Rains
RE	Reading
RJ	Ray Jones
RL	Roger Latham
RO	Robin Ollington
ROB	Robert Thompson
RR	Rupert Redway
RS	Royston Robertson
RT	Richard Tomes
RU	Russell
SA	Sally Artz
SE	Stan Eales
SM	Sam Smith
SP	Spittle
ST	Stan
STP	Stamp
SW	Steve Way
TA	Alexey Talimonov
TH	Tony Husband
WA	Waldorf
WAR	Warner
WC	Woodcock
WI	Wilbur
WR	Wren

'I'm going on strike to wear trousers'